Find the Truth!

Everything you are about to read is true *except* for one of the sentences on this page.

Which one is **TRUE**?

T or F Several battles took place in New York during the Revolutionary War.

T or F The English were the first Europeans to settle what became New York.

Find the answers in this book.

Contents

**General Washington and
the Continental army**

THE **BIG** TRUTH!

New York's Founding Fathers

William Floyd

The Dutch West
India Company brought
11 slaves to New
Netherland in 1625.

Timeline of New York Colony History

1500s

Native Americans live throughout New York

1624

New Amsterdam is founded.

1683

The colony's General Assembly is created.

1775

American colonists fight first battles with the British.

1788

New York ratifies the U.S. Constitution.

CHAPTER 1

The Native Americans

The area of present-day New York has been home to many Native American peoples. Groups such as the Mohawk, Oneida, and Seneca shared the **Iroquois** language and many aspects of their everyday lives. Five Mahican groups lived in areas around today's Hudson River. The Lenni-Lenape inhabited a region that stretched from southern New York to Delaware. The Lenni-Lenape and Mahicans spoke languages of the **Algonquian** family.

Finding Food, Growing Food

Many of the region's Native Americans hunted, fished, and gathered wild plants. Some also farmed. Farmers planted maize (corn), beans, and squash. Hunters used short spears and bows to hunt deer, turkey, and rabbit. People living near water used

Hunting was mostly done by men.

traps, nets, and bone hooks to catch salmon and trout. Women gathered herbs, berries, and other plants. These plants were used for food and medicine.

Iroquois referred to their alliance as the *Haudenosaunee* (HO-den-oh-SHO-nee). ➡

The Great Peacemaker convinced the five Iroquois groups to set aside their differences and join together.

"People of the Longhouse"

The Iroquois peoples once quarreled with one another over hunting grounds and sites for villages. The Great Peacemaker and the gifted speaker Ayenwatha (ah-yon-WAT-ha) joined to convince the Iroquois to end their disputes. They encouraged the Iroquois to form an **alliance** against their enemies. The Iroquois had banded together into the "people of the longhouse" by the 1500s. This name was a reference to the timber and sod homes built by Iroquois groups.

Area enlarged

Original 13 Colonies

miles 100

km 100

CANADA

St. Lawrence River

Lake Champlain

Adirondack Mountains

VERMONT
(CLAIMED BY
NEW HAMPSHIRE
AND NEW YORK)

Fort Ticonderoga

Lake Ontario

Fort Oswego

Fort Stanwix

NEW HAMPSHIRE

Lake Erie

S E N E C A

O N O N D A G A

O N E I D A

M O H A W K

Mohawk River

• Saratoga

Albany •

Hudson River

MASSACHUSETTS

NEW YORK

Catskill Mountains

• Kingston

CONNECTICUT

New Paltz •

• Poughkeepsie

PENNSYLVANIA

Appalachian Mountains

Delaware River

Susquehanna River

Long Island

New Amsterdam
(New York) •

• Brooklyn

Colonial boundaries

Present boundaries

L E N N I L E N A R E

NEW JERSEY

ATLANTIC OCEAN

MARYLAND

DELAWARE

VIRGINIA

CHAPTER 2

The Settlers

The Lenni-Lenape first encountered Europeans in the early or mid-1500s. English explorer Henry Hudson landed on what became Manhattan Island in 1609. Hudson was working for a Dutch company. He traded with the local peoples before sailing up today's Hudson River. Hudson sent reports of fine farmland and friendly Indian traders. This convinced the Dutch West India Company to start a colony in the area. They named the colony New Netherland.

New Amsterdam

Thirty Dutch families set up four settlements in the colony in 1624. The main village of New Amsterdam was located on the southern tip of Manhattan. More settlers arrived the next year. A new colony leader named Peter Minuit arrived in 1626. He bought Manhattan from local Native Americans, possibly for tools, cloth, kettles, and other items. This expanded New Amsterdam. The Dutch began clearing land to build farms and a new town.

Henry Hudson explored New York for the Netherlands.

Henry Hudson's ship was named the *Half Moon*.

The Dutch settlers built towns along waterways.

Traders from the Netherlands bought beaver
and otter furs from the Indians. The furs were
used to make and sell expensive hats and clothing
in Europe. The Lenni-Lenape received metal tools
and pots in return. These were highly prized items.
The Algonquian peoples lacked access to metal
products at the time.

Peter Minuit

Peter Minuit was born in the German town of
Wesel in 1580. His purchase of Manhattan remains
a famous moment in American history. Historians
believe the Native Americans sold Minuit the right
to use the island, not to keep it forever. Minuit was
fired by the Dutch West India Company in 1632.
But he continued to work in the Americas. In 1638,
he led Swedish colonists in settling New Sweden,
in present-day Delaware.

Different Dutch fur companies also competed with one another for the American Indians' business.

Fur Wars

The fur trade created conflict among the Native Americans. The Mohawk wanted to drive the Mahican out of the Hudson River region and take control of all trade with the Dutch. The fighting between the two peoples spilled over into attacks on settlers and traders. The Dutch feared attack. They built a wooden barrier around New Amsterdam. The Mohawk victory brought a brief peace. But it was followed by years of bad leadership and bloody conflict with the Lenni-Lenape.

The Stuyvesant Years

The Dutch West India Company turned to former soldier Peter Stuyvesant to lead New Amsterdam in 1647. Stuyvesant immediately passed laws to clean up the colony. Fences, buildings, the local windmill, and the town fort underwent repairs. Workers paved New Amsterdam's streets with stones. They also built a protective wall along Wall Street. Stuyvesant also organized a police force to deal with the town's crime.

New York City's Bowery neighborhood is named after Peter Stuyvesant's farm.

Peter Stuyvesant brought major changes to the New Amsterdam colony.

Stuyvesant greatly improved conditions in New Amsterdam. But he made enemies. The taxes he placed on furs and other products to pay for the colony's improvements were unpopular. He also ran into opposition to his ideas on religion. New

Many Quaker settlers came to New Amsterdam.

Amsterdam was unlike most colonies. It accepted people of any faith. But Stuyvesant tried to exclude Jews, Quakers, and others. The Dutch West India Company forced him to allow such groups to settle. But Stuyvesant refused to let them worship outside their own homes.

The English arrived in New York's harbor in 1664.

England Takes Over

England controlled colonies along the Atlantic Coast. It decided to add New Amsterdam to its holdings. English soldiers met no resistance from colonists when they first arrived. Dutch colonists soon agreed to officially give power over the colony to England if colonists could continue trading and living as they had. New Netherland became New York. New Amsterdam was renamed New York City. Stuyvesant stayed and lived as an ordinary citizen on his nearby farm.

Wanting a Voice

The Dutch government tried for several years to take back control of the colony. But they made their final surrender to England in 1674. Thomas Dongan was the English governor of the colony in 1683. He allowed New Yorkers to create a **legislature** called the General Assembly. Only male landowners and businessmen could vote. That same year the assembly passed laws guaranteeing rights to the colonists such as free speech and trial by jury. The Duke of York, the English noble who owned New York, gave his approval.

The Dutch temporarily regained control of New York in 1673 before surrendering it in 1674.

James II took the throne on February 6, 1685.

James II ruled for just a few years before being replaced during a revolution.

The duke became King James II in 1685. He combined New York with other nearby colonies into a single colony called the Dominion of New England. But the change lasted only until James was replaced as king in 1688. New York returned to being its own colony. Colonists in New York City captured the British soldiers there and elected Jacob Leisler governor.

Leisler's Changes

Leisler allowed many of the poor to vote. Many tradesmen, farmers, and store owners supported him. But rich landowners and merchants did not. English soldiers returned to New York City in 1691 and defeated a local **militia**. Leisler was put on trial and hanged as a traitor. Some of Leisler's changes remained in place. They reminded New Yorkers that they could have a voice in their own government.

Jacob Leisler became governor of New York after James was replaced as the British monarch by William and Mary.

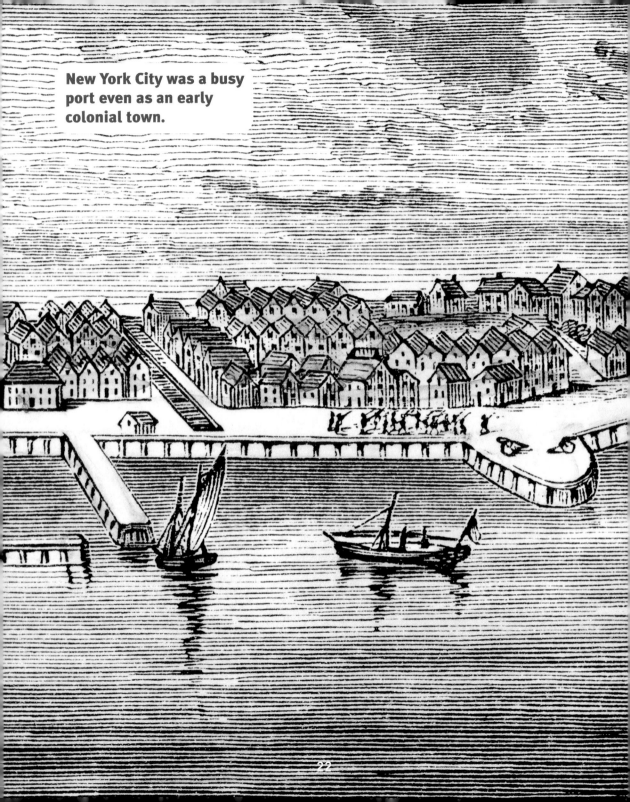

New York City was a busy port even as an early colonial town.

Living in the Colony

New York offered colonists a wide variety of work possibilities. The merchants who got rich from the fur trade began to be replaced by traders who dealt in lumber and many other products. Educated professionals such as lawyers and accountants began to establish numerous businesses throughout New York City.

 Today, New York City has the largest population of any city in the United States.

William Bradford owned a bookstore in Philadelphia.

William Bradford's publications inspired political discussion in New York City.

The city's prosperity also helped boost a tradesman's chances of success. Printer William Bradford published books and a popular newspaper called the *New-York Gazette*. Carpenters, masons, and bricklayers built homes and churches for the wealthy. These tradesmen could often afford to erect houses for themselves. Goods brought in by merchants allowed New Yorkers to open shops with the latest products from the colonies and England.

Wealthy women in New York City could afford to buy expensive clothes and to hire servants.

The Colony's Women

Women could keep their own names and buy land during the days of Dutch control. They could also pass this land to their children. But the English ended these freedoms. Most women in New York worked in the home. They took care of children, made clothes, and cooked. Some made items such as candles to sell. Some unmarried women helped with family businesses or worked as servants for the wealthy.

Going to School

Stuyvesant valued education. New York had more schools than many other colonies. Dutch children had a six-hour school day. Children were taught math, reading, writing, and religion. Some teachers punished misbehavior by hitting students with willow branches. Others forced students to sit on sharp tacks. Girls usually sat in the back of the classroom. Children on farms had to help with chores when they were not in school.

Most colonial schools only had one classroom.

In 1703, 42 percent of New York's homes had slaves.

Slaves

The Dutch slave trade was small compared to the southern colonies'. They also granted some rights to slaves. Free blacks were slaves who had arrived on Dutch ships. They were allowed to own property. The Dutch also kept slaves in half-slavery. They were forced to work but could later be freed. New York slaves still did not have the same rights and freedoms as their owners.

England had a harsher view of slavery. Britain regained control in 1664. Free blacks lost the right to own property in 1712. The English encouraged slave trading because of the huge profits.

New York City was an important trade center during the French and Indian War.

28

CHAPTER 4

Fighting for Independence

Great Britain and France went to war for control of North America in 1754. The French and Indian War led to attacks on British settlements in northern New York by pro-French Native Americans. New York City became a base for British ships and soldiers. New Yorkers sold supplies and products to the British military as the war continued.

⬅ The French and Indian War is also called the Seven Years' War.

Even as the British celebrated an end to war with France, trouble was brewing in its colonies across the Atlantic.

Paying for Victory

Britain defeated France in 1760. The two sides signed a peace treaty three years later. New York's economy suffered with Britain's military gone. Britain had borrowed huge amounts of money to fight the war and build forts. Parliament, the British legislature, decided to tax its American colonies to help pay for the war. The colonists complained about the first new taxes. The Stamp Act of 1765 caused anger and protests.

The Stamp Act

The Stamp Act stated that colonists had to buy a British stamp to place on paper materials such as newspapers and legal documents. This angered the colonists. A mob destroyed the governor's house in New York City. Another mob surrounded the fort that stored the stamps. Merchants throughout the colonies placed a **boycott** on British goods. British businesses pressured Parliament to cancel the Stamp Act in 1766.

Stamps were a common form of taxation throughout Great Britain.

Angry colonists took to the streets to protest the Stamp Act.

Unfair Taxes

Colonists did not oppose all taxes. They paid taxes to colonial governments. But laws such as the Stamp Act angered colonists because they had no one to represent their interests in Parliament and to argue against taxes. They called this "taxation without representation." Antitax organizations and anti-British groups such as the Sons of Liberty organized to protest unfair acts by the British government.

Some protests became violent.

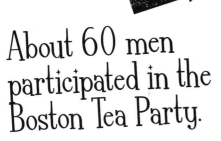

About 60 men participated in the Boston Tea Party.

The tea protests in Boston and New York destroyed 342 chests of tea.

Tea Tax Trouble

A tax on tea added to the cost of a drink enjoyed by colonists everywhere. Colonists became even angrier when Parliament allowed a British company to sell tea tax-free while continuing to force American companies to pay the tax. The Sons of Liberty dumped British tea into Boston Harbor in December 1773. This event became known as the Boston Tea Party. New Yorkers did the same in their city the following April.

War in the Colonies

The colonies asked King George III of Britain for fairer treatment in 1774. **Patriots** also boycotted British goods. Both actions failed to bring about change. British soldiers searching for ammunition and other supplies hidden by colonists fought Massachusetts militia at Lexington and Concord in April 1775. The colonies' Continental army was led by George Washington. It gathered near Boston to battle Britain's forces. The American Revolutionary War had begun.

The Continental army did not have the training or the resources of the British military.

Most of the British troops were asleep when American militia first entered Fort Ticonderoga.

The American forces seized Fort Ticonderoga on May 10, 1775.

Ticonderoga

Much of the early Revolutionary War took place in and around New York. Patriot Ethan Allen and American officer Benedict Arnold led the Green Mountain Boys' militia to victory over British soldiers at Fort Ticonderoga in May 1775. The fort provided cannons and gunpowder that the desperate Continental army used to fight the British in Boston in 1776. The British then turned the might of their army upon New York City.

Retreat From New York

Five hundred British ships appeared off Long Island in July 1776. **Loyalists** joined British forces at the Battle of Long Island the next month. The Continental army was driven back to Manhattan. It holed up until the British again landed thousands of troops in October. The Continentals fell back again. They left behind mountains of supplies. A fire swept through part of the city behind them as they retreated.

The British were victorious at the Battle of Long Island.

British forces took 1,200 American prisoners at the Battle of Long Island.

Escape on Long Island

The British almost destroyed the Continental army in 1776. Washington had placed troops on a series of hills across Long Island. Area Loyalists told the British commanders of a way to sneak around the hills. The panicked Americans barely managed to retreat to forts in Brooklyn. There, the much larger enemy forces trapped them against the East River. Washington saved his army with a daring late-night retreat across the river.

New York's Founding Fathers

Twelve colonies sent representatives to the First Continental Congress in 1774. But King George III ignored their request for respect and better treatment. A Second Continental Congress met in May 1775 to decide how to resolve the colonies' problems with Britain. Many representatives had no plans to break away from British rule at first. But more representatives favored **independence** by spring 1776. The congress voted for the Declaration of Independence on July 2. Four New Yorkers signed the document. Here are three of them.

William Floyd

William Floyd's family had lived in New York since the 1650s. He served in the militia and in the Continental Congress during the war. He became a member of the U.S. House of Representatives in 1789.

Philip Livingston

Philip Livingston actively protested the Stamp Act of 1765. He also argued for independence in the Second Continental Congress. He served in New York's state government and the Continental Congress until his sudden death in 1778.

Lewis Morris

Lewis Morris was related to many Revolutionary War figures. His half-brother, Gouverneur, wrote parts of the U.S. Constitution. Morris served in New York's state government for many years. He cast a vote in favor of the Constitution in 1788.

Upstate Fighting

British forces from Canada, Lake Ontario, and Manhattan attacked American troops in the Hudson River valley in early 1777. British general John Burgoyne led his invasion force down Lake Champlain and took back Fort Ticonderoga. But Continentals and local farmers kept up pressure with quick attacks and hit-and-run raids as Burgoyne's troops continued south. The fighting ended with a British surrender at Saratoga.

The American victory at Saratoga was a major turning point in the Revolutionary War.

American forces took about 8,000 British prisoners at Yorktown.

The conflict at Yorktown was the last major battle of the American Revolutionary War.

The battered Continental forces were becoming convinced they could defeat the mighty British army. Washington had moved close to New York City by 1779. But he could not regain it. The British lost a major battle at Yorktown, Virginia, in October 1781. They surrendered to the Americans. The war was over. Britain withdrew the last of its troops from New York City on November 25, 1783. Washington led Continental soldiers into the city.

The U.S. Constitution

Colonists split in the 1780s over whether or not the new country needed a strong national government. Twelve states sent representatives to a convention in Philadelphia in 1787 to work out a **constitution** that would create a new government. The U.S. Constitution went to each state for a vote after months of debate. New York approved it in 1788. It became the 11th state of the United States. ★

New York was one of the last to approve the Constitution.

55 representatives helped to create the U.S. Constitution.

True Statistics

Number of Iroquois peoples in the original alliance: 5

Number of families who began New Netherland: 30

Number of New Amsterdam settlers in 1647: About 700

Population of New York Colony in 1700: 20,000

Number of wars fought between Britain and France for North America: 4

Number of British soldiers at Fort Ticonderoga: About 50

Year British soldiers left New York City: 1783

Number of New Yorkers who signed the Declaration of Independence: 4

Did you find the truth?

T Several battles took place in New York during the Revolutionary War.

F The English were the first Europeans to settle what became New York.

Resources

Books

Cotter, Kristin. *New York*. New York: Children's Press, 2008.

Dalton, Anne. *The Lenape of Pennsylvania, New Jersey, New York, Delaware, Wisconsin, Oklahoma, and Ontario*. New York: PowerKids, 2005.

Gibson, Karen B. *New Netherland*. Hockessin, DE: Mitchell Lane, 2007.

Ingram, Scott. *The Battle of Long Island*. San Diego: Blackbirch Press, 2004.

January, Brendan. *Colonial Life*. New York: Children's Press, 2001.

St. Lawrence, Genevieve. *The Iroquois and Their History*. Mankato, MN: Compass Point, 2006.

Takacs, Stefanie. *The Iroquois*. New York: Children's Press, 2003.

Whiting, Jim. *Peter Stuyvesant*. Hockessin, DE: Mitchell Lane, 2008.

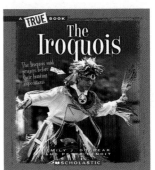

Organizations and Web Sites

Museum of the City of New York

www.mcny.org

See online exhibits on Henry Hudson, look at old maps, and learn about the history of New York from the days of the Lenni-Lenape to today.

New-York Historical Society

www.nyhistory.org/web

Explore an online archive of photographs, art, maps, and other materials related to the history of New York.

Places to Visit

Fort Ticonderoga

100 Fort Road
Ticonderoga, NY 12883
(518) 585-2821
www.fort-ticonderoga.org
Visit the site of this Revolutionary War battle and learn about what happened through exhibits and reenactments.

New York State Museum

222 Madison Avenue
Albany, NY 12230
(518) 474-5877
www.nysm.nysed.gov
Wander the many exhibits of this museum to learn the history of New York's Native Americans, settlers, and other people.

Important Words

Algonquian (al-GON-kwin)—a group of Native American peoples that once lived across eastern North America

alliance (uh-LYE-uhns)—an agreement to work together for some result

boycott (BOI-kaht)—refusing to buy goods from a person, group, or country

constitution (kahn-sti-TOO-shun)—the laws of a country that state the rights of the people and the powers of government

independence (in-di-PEN-duhns)—a state of not being controlled by others

Iroquois (EER-uh-kwoi)—a group of Native American peoples that once lived across eastern North America

legislature (LEJ-is-lay-chur)—a group of people who have the power to make or change laws

Loyalists (LOI-uhl-ists)—American colonists who remained faithful to Great Britain

militia (muh-LISH-uh)—a group of people who are trained to fight but who aren't professional soldiers

Patriots (PAY-tree-uhts)—American colonists opposed to Great Britain

Index

Page numbers in **bold** indicate illustrations

About the Author

Kevin Cunningham has written more than 40 books on disasters, the history of disease, Native Americans, and other topics. Cunningham lives near Chicago with his wife and young daughter.